Michael Prentice lives in North Devon. He grew up here and has returned in recent years. Having spent a large part of his life away, attending Warwick University, living in the West Midlands; living and working in London for 12 years and a year respectively living in both the USA and in Spain – he has finally returned to roost!

Michael is also currently having his next two books published by Austin Macauley – these are entitled *Antiques Antics* and *Corruption in the Met* and he is currently just completing his fifth book which is a novel entitled *The Canterbury Express*. So look out for these soon!

I dedicate this book to each of my family members – you know who you are and what we all had to go through individually and together. Our mutual support gave us the strength to endure this.

The book is especially devoted to Sarah for whom it will serve as an account of that part of her life which saw her grow up strong as a young woman.

The book also aims to serve as a helping hand to those who have to go through this... in the hope that it gives you strength.

I give thanks and praise to God for giving us the outcome that we so needed.

# Michael Prentice

# Staring Death in the Face

AUSTIN MACAULEY PUBLISHERS™

LONDON • CAMBRIDGE • NEW YORK • SHARJAH

Copyright © Michael Prentice 2022

The right of Michael Prentice to be identified as author of this work has been asserted by the author in accordance with sections 77 and 78 of the Copyright, Designs and Patents Act 1988.

All rights reserved. No part of this publication may be reproduced, stored in a retrieval system, or transmitted in any form or by any means, electronic, mechanical, photocopying, recording, or otherwise, without the prior permission of the publishers.

Any person who commits any unauthorised act in relation to this publication may be liable to criminal prosecution and civil claims for damages.

A CIP catalogue record for this title is available from the British Library.

ISBN 9781398476813 (Paperback)
ISBN 9781398476820 (ePub e-book)

www.austinmacauley.com

First Published 2022
Austin Macauley Publishers Ltd®
1 Canada Square
Canary Wharf
London
E14 5AA

It began in the summer of 2012. Only now have I been able to face writing this book, some nine years later.

# 1
# Talented

Sarah, our daughter was in year ten at school, she was 14 years old at the time. She was doing very well there, not just academically but in sports too, theatre and drama etc. I recall her first days of senior school where we had to drive her in instead of her taking the school bus, as she had broken her toes in three places after her over-exuberance in a village playground. A high-achiever, Sarah would always want to do well in all of her subjects and all that she did. Ever since primary school, she had wanted to and achieved very high and usually did.

She would attain a full set of straight A's or A stars across all of her subjects. As a parent, attending her parent's evenings at school was always rewarding and it made you so proud to hear that Sarah was often top of the class in just about almost everything she was doing.

During her final year of junior school, here in North Devon, she had been chosen for the part of Eliza Doolittle, the lead role in the school play *My Fair Lady*. She played the role fantastically and with an astonishing, real cockney accent. She received standing ovations from the Landmark Theatre, Ilfracombe audience where it was performed. Other parents turned to us, as her parents, in the audience as the curtain went up giving us nods, thumbs-up and smiles of approval. I remember the head teacher running out speedily to go and find Sarah after the final curtain had lowered, saying, "Where's Sarah? She stole the show and held it all together wonderfully for us…where is she, I must congratulate her." Parents came up to us saying all and the same thing…We were so proud of her. She really had 'stolen the show'.

Was she striving maybe just a little bit too hard continually to achieve these high standards and academic school results which had now become something of her trademark? We, as her parents, were beginning to ask ourselves this question as we were noticing that she had become quite thin of late, maybe thinner than we had seen her before. Was she putting too much effort in and strain on herself? Too much strain to keep up all the high achievements…and pushing herself just a little bit too hard in the process…

# 2

# Changes in the Kitchen, Sarah Takes Control

It was no exaggeration to say that recently the contents of the cupboards in our kitchen had undergone a dramatic transformation, not in the sense that the shelves had undergone a physical renovation or anything like that but that the cupboards' contents were experiencing something of an overhaul. The shelves were now starting to fill with considerably healthier foods than before. Packs of dried cranberries were appearing, sesame seed snack bars, almond flakes, mixed-seeds packs and strawberry yoghurt flake packets were not just appearing but were beginning to abound. Lightly salted wholegrain low-fat rice cakes, which were so light that you might very well have thought they would blow out of your hand and away in the breeze if there had been one – these had now become the order of the day and were seemingly taking over from what I would only describe as 'ordinary foods'. Tins of tuna flakes, too many tins of tuna flakes, were now newly being neatly stacked up in rows filling up the cupboard shelves. Still, tuna flakes are quite nice!

Gone now were the jars of mayonnaise, pickles, packs of hand-baked crisps, bars of chocolate and fudge and the fridge too was becoming noticeably and painfully short of our favourite sausages, salami and store-baked ready-made pizzas.

I was aware of loose conversations I had previously with Claire my wife about looking at 'what we ate' in order to become healthier as a family and I'd agreed to that but had no idea we would be taking such drastic action in so short a space of time in order to achieve this.

Sarah had become the main player in this rapid and dramatic kitchen cupboard transformation. She would always somehow almost instinctively seem to know when Mum was getting ready to prepare dinner for the family and would always appear in the kitchen at exactly the right time ready to take charge of proceedings. A good old-fashioned steak and chips was now becoming a thing of the past in our house. Gone now seemed to be the days of a good meat pie and mash. No more were we being served sausages, egg, chips and beans; that wonderful man's dinner favourite! What's going on?

When dinner was up, we came to a table which was now displaying largely salad ingredients. Salad with salad and more salad on top! What is happening in our household? A man can't live on that!

Sarah was now also appearing to be the main organiser of the family dinner; her roles now were seemingly that of a shopping-list writer, preparer of food, and overseer of all that went on in the kitchen. She was taking control especially at serving up time too. It was head chef Sarah in the kitchen. Mum seemed to be taken in with all this and just went along with it.

Salads had become the bulk of the daily meal, salad, salad and...salad! Food portions too had become somewhat smaller. A man really can't live with that!

# 3
# Before the End of Summer Term

We had a lovely black Labrador dog called Freddy. Although becoming quite an elderly statesman by now, our daily walks with Freddy included walks over the surrounding farmland fields and lanes next to our edge of Exmoor home. Sarah would always want to come for the dog walk. She had shed a lot of weight lately and now something odd and awful was happening to her as she had started to get what I can only describe as 'rolling eyes syndrome'. I noticed to my obvious alarm that her eyes would roll upwards and back in her head showing the whites of her eyes as we walked along. I had never seen anything quite like it before and was naturally very worried about it. She was also looking quite pale, gaunt and generally unwell. Without fail, she would always want to get involved in all aspects of any physical exercise going on in the family, never was a dog walk missed! Afternoons of family badminton at the local leisure centre and Sarah was always first to be there. We had all noticed her considerable weight loss, had gently prodded her in this area without seemingly any notice being taken and we discussed this amongst ourselves as a family, almost as a self-help counselling group, a great deal. The fuss she made at meal times over every little thing she ate or rather didn't eat; small morsels hidden under vegetable leaves so as not to be seen; the playing around with food on the plate making it look as if she was actually eating it but wasn't; serving up food to everyone else but herself. What kind of charade was this?

We were very worried. As a Christian family, we prayed. She had become quite painfully thin. What was going on with her? Surely she could see the change herself in the mirror; mirrors don't lie.

Was this…dare I say it…anorexia?

# 4

# Summer Trip to Denia

That summer I had to go to Denia in Spain where we had a small bungalow near the coast which we were fortunate to have as a holiday home and which we sometimes rented out. I was going to go alone for a week to do a few odd maintenance jobs at the place that needed doing...a bit of painting and maintenance work here and there before the new summer season began once again. Sarah wanted to come with me. I was so in two minds about taking her because of her having lost too much weight but she pleaded with me to come and told me adamantly that she would eat well and that I shouldn't worry and all would be fine. I had huge reservations about this and largely against my will and instinct I bowed to her pressure and let her come along with me.

It was 'far from fine!' Sarah just simply wouldn't eat anything much at all; just a few salad bits here and there mainly and she and I came to a crossroads there in Spain. I told her in no uncertain terms that if she didn't start to eat properly, I would be taking her to the airport and get her flown back home to England early. I argued with her to eat. She in turn lied to me that she had eaten something earlier already, which I pretty much knew was nonsense. This continued day after day. Exasperated, I was then on the telephone with Claire, my wife and she said that she would look into earlier flights back home for Sarah. Sarah bawled out that she didn't want to have to go home early.

There was another issue now that a young 15-year-old girl, like Sarah, would need to be accompanied by an adult on a flight as she was too young to fly on her own! We didn't know of anyone who would be able to accompany her now at such short notice and we had to concede that we couldn't do anything about the dilemma at such a late time into the break now. I was stuck with the problem and Sarah would have to stay with me for the remaining days. She was piling a ton of stress on me at a time when I could really have done with her help! I was very agitated with her now about the whole ridiculous ongoing predicament which she was putting me and the rest of the family through so unnecessarily! Clearly, she was anorexic and this would have to be addressed head-on once we were home. Not only was she killing herself but she was also killing me!

# 5
# Bous A La Mar

**Bous a la Mar** – in Denia, Spain (This literally translated means 'Bulls by the Sea')

Bous a la Mar is a festival where, as part of the summer bull-running and bull-fighting fiestas in Spain, they have an arena right next to the open sea wall edge in Denia where brave, if not slightly daft, men line up against this wall whilst the arena bulls are let loose and charge at them. The brave/daft men can try to stand up to the bulls like matadors, or run away, or dive into the sea, oftentimes with the bulls jumping in the water after them. It is a crazy fiesta often marked by injuries to the men (we have seen some quite horrendous sights there). I went along with Sarah to this spectacle and quite frankly can honestly say how embarrassed I was by all the looks of concern, disgust and disbelief that were directed at Sarah and us by the public everywhere, at her distressing, sorry physical state. People would look at her and us, mutter some things and as you turned around having passed them, you could see them still staring back in disbelief. Sarah was just as much a spectacle to people as the bull-ring was. She was alarmingly thin now. I was very cross with her as not only was she spoiling my break away in Spain but she was heaping stress onto my shoulders at a time when I really needed the opposite through her continually exacerbating the problem for us all by refusing to eat. More arguments ensued between Sarah and me. It was an unpleasant stay though it should not have been so. Sarah had gone against her every word to me! I called her 'anorexic' but she flatly denied it, seeming not to like this term. To most people, she clearly was clearly anorexic!

At the end of the week, I was relieved to finally get Sarah home alive and to get home myself; no nice break at all!

# 6
# Back to School

Soon summer holidays were coming to an end and it was time to resume back at school. We were all worried for Sarah and not least because her illness was bound to be noticed by everyone at her school; tutors and classmates alike which would bring about lots of questions.

She went to our GP. Anorexia was diagnosed and they were concerned about her condition but said she was still well enough to attend school. Surprising, the GP said she was even fit to take part in school sports which I was very amazed at, such a ridiculous decision which I challenged and upon doing so the GP 'changed his mind' within days and then disallowed her from taking part in all sports. Thank goodness for that…for Sarah's sake!

Questions were immediately asked of Sarah as to her health by the school and Claire and I were called in and see the headmaster to explain. In order to protect Sarah, as a dad would, and with believing to have her best interests at heart, I tried to downplay the severity of her predicament. I told the headmaster that although Sarah had been dramatically trying to lose weight, she had also had a bad virus which had also contributed to her weight loss. This was not the truth but we had agreed beforehand as a family that we would do everything we could to protect Sarah, her future and her best interests; from her getting behind in her studies and to her being asked to leave that good school.

Sarah somehow continued to survive on mice-sized food portions until school half-term holiday break.

# 7
# Autumn Half Term in Okehampton

During the half-term holiday break, our family went to stay at a really lovely self-catering holiday accommodation at East Hook, near Okehampton on the edge of Dartmoor. We had stayed here before and really enjoyed it so had returned for more adventures. Pictures on the wall there showed that we were following in the footsteps of some well-known personalities, as both Bill Oddie and Kate Humble (Naturalist) had stayed here before us! We went Dartmoor Tor walking and played fun games in the nearby park. Sarah was still pushing herself physically whilst in her complete state of denial as to her awful physical and mental condition and stubbornly would not change her ways. She even ran in her attempts to be the first up the Dartmoor Tors and went climbing on the climbing wall at the park.

Sarah on the climbing wall at Simmons Park, Okehampton whilst seriously unwell.

She was so gaunt and ill-looking now that looking at her was like staring death in the face! We could not literally force food down into her mouth but I must admit there were times when I considered it, with the alternative being that we were onlookers simply watching our own daughter slowly killing herself.

We had lots of heartache and conversations with the rest of the family. We prayed a great deal daily and we resolved to take her back to the doctor when we got back, which we did.

The half-term holiday came and went and it was now time to go back to school. The big question was now whether Sarah was actually well enough to attend?

Claire had seen Sarah screaming out in pain on a few occasions at our house as the pain of her own body now shutting down became excruciating for her. To protect Sarah and I from this she would pretend to me that nothing much had just happened – that Sarah had just stubbed her toe or suchlike!

Her hair was now falling out in noticeable clumps and she could die at any moment. Sarah just looked like 'death' itself! To me as a Christian, I could see a spirit of death all over her. The devil had gotten a firm hold of her and was going to try to pull her down. Satan was doing all he could to destroy and bring down this Christian family, to tear us apart irredeemably. I was going to do all I could to prevent this and spoke directly at Sarah casting the devil off her in the "name of Jesus". On one occasion whilst standing in our kitchen doing this, Sarah shouted at me and made a sort of unusual demonic moaning noise back in my direction. I was looking straight at the demon of death and loosening its grip on her in the name of Jesus Christ and we continued to pray earnestly as a family for her to somehow pull through.

Unbelievably, our GP said that she was okay to continue at school but that they were now very concerned about her. They would be referring her to see the mental health specialists. Thank goodness at last!

# 8
# Time to Face School Again

She went back to school to face embarrassing comments at school from the other girls. A mixed bag of comments from genuine concern to unhelpful remarks directed at her but what did she really expect?

Shortly after, Sarah was referred to the hospital and CAMHS (Child and Adult Mental Health Services) team in North Devon.

Going back to school lasted for just a week...before full hospital admission.

# 9

# On the Brink

Upon seeing the specialists in Devon, both at the hospital and at the CAMHS offices, Sarah was hurried to the hospital. The CAMHS team in particular were alarmed at how it had taken so long for Sarah to be admitted to their services. They told us that standard GP's often don't know much of what they were talking about when it came to anorexia. I had already made a complaint about our GP to this effect.

We were now told that Sarah was the worst case child anorexic that they had ever encountered in terms of her body mass weight. She was so light in weight that her body was shutting down and she was now at death's door. Meetings with the paediatrician specialist at the hospital and the CAMHS team were difficult and tense as we as parents had reservations as to the old-fashioned techniques that we believed they still employed in treating mental health patients. There appeared to be something of an antiquated 'One flew over the Cuckoo's Nest' mentality, rather than bringing mental health a little more into the twenty-first century we felt and in treating each individual a little more respectfully and individually as people.

Perhaps we were a little biased because we were dealing with our own daughter in this horrendous predicament. Perhaps not!

Sarah still appeared to be in denial. In all honesty, I think we too as her parents were also a little in denial as we couldn't really fathom what was occurring here to our daughter, who had been perfectly healthy one moment but by her own doing was now suddenly right at death's door.

Sarah was admitted to the hospital initially for a few weeks. She was very fortunate to be given her own private ward to give her personal privacy and be away from prying eyes, which was really a blessing for her.

We visited her every day on her ward and Claire and I went literally every single day to see her.

On one occasion, Sarah phoned me from the hospital crying profusely to tell me that the ward nurse had accused her of scraping the butter off her breakfast toast with her knife and hidden it on the underside of her plate so that it wouldn't be noticed (a common trait of anorexics apparently), so once again I tried to believe Sarah as my daughter at this time was telling me the truth and I complained to the hospital to "leave Sarah alone". This began a difficult interaction between us as parents and the hospital ward. I, as Sarah's father, was caught between not knowing really whether to believe my own daughter on the one hand and trying to defend and protect her on the other! It was an impossible position to find myself in and one I was very unhappy being in. The stress was an unbearable load.

With the CAMHS team too, I had previously heard mixed reports about how good they actually were. Apparently, they are a charity organisation and from the start, I didn't get along very well with Sarah's assigned 'helper'. Again, in all honesty and with hindsight, we think it was probably us who were partly the problem, still perhaps being in a partial state of non-acceptance of it all.

# 10
# The Odd Hospital Consultant

Sarah's specialist consultant, Dr Crook was a very difficult man to deal with, however. A plainly arrogant individual whom later we found out had been found guilty of a criminal offence at the hospital, who was conditionally discharged and then later was suspended further by the hospital because another offence against him was being investigated. We have no idea whether he was later readmitted back into the hospital or not. Hopefully not!

From the beginning, he tried to claim personal credit continually for each ounce of weight that Sarah slowly began to put back on, to the point of nausea!

He told Sarah that if she gained a certain weight within the first two weeks of her admission then he would let her come home; this was a challenge to Sarah as she did not want to be there and seemingly the penny was just beginning to drop with her as she amazingly began to gain small portions of weight and so having reached her target after the two weeks, we went to fetch her. On entering the hospital, we got Sarah's things together to bring her home and we were just leaving the hospital when this awful Doctor came along.

"Where do you think you are going?" said Doctor Crook.

"We're taking Sarah back home now as you advised," I replied.

"Well, I don't think she's lost enough weight yet for you to do that!" Crook replied.

"You told us quite clearly that if she lost the weight you stated then she was fit to come home," I said as we continued to walk on towards the hospital ward lift.

He followed us and said, "No, you can't leave."

I said, "We're only doing what you advised us and we've come all this way now and are ready to go." And by now, we were standing at the open lift door.

Typically arrogant, Dr Crook stood at the lift door and put his foot in the door so as not to allow it to close.

I said, "Alright, we'll take the stairs in that case then." And we walked out of the lift and around to the stairs and left the hospital.

"I won't allow this," he called on behind us.

"We're just doing as you advised," I repeated.

We just left, having had enough of this man and I sought to make a complaint about him as soon as we got home.

In many ways, we were too late for that it seemed, as on our way back home, we passed a police car parked up near to our home. I half-jokingly said to our family, "Perhaps that Doctor Crook has sent them after us!"

It really turned out to be no joke in reality as that's exactly what had happened and the doctor had stitched us up by telling the police that we had removed Sarah from the ward against his advice and that we now found ourselves in contravention of the law! There was a message from the police on my phone by the time we made it home and we were now in a position of being legally compelled to return Sarah to the ward. It was an invidious scenario created completely by the arrogant Doctor Crook. We returned Sarah to the ward where ironically she had to spend only two more days solely at the whims and fancy of that arrogant doctor.

The great sign though was that Sarah was beginning to gain small amounts of weight. But she was far from being out of the woods yet.

# 11

# Home Again

Once home, she made concerted efforts to gain some weight but it was a painstakingly slow process. She 'picked' so fussily at all of her food that it was alarming to watch. Still, as the weeks rolled by and into months and with continued visits to odd doctor, she gradually became more than a shadow of her former self again. Claire was particularly patient with Sarah and gave her a lot of space to manoeuvre so to speak. I was somewhat less patient I'm afraid and we were all still struggling to come to terms with the family's ordeal. I saw each of our family members in tears from one moment to the next with our self-help counselling group going on between us.

What a cruel thing this eating disorder is, not just for the person themselves but for the family around them having to look on helplessly, not knowing which way to turn…with 50-50 odds at best! But worse still knowing that anorexia is a kind of long drawn out form of suicide…really it is one of the worst things that can happen to a family!

But Sarah was still alive…this was a miracle in itself…and how close she had come to death. By the grace of God, she was still with us. Thank you, God! Praise God for saving Sarah and for rescuing this family from a lifetime of unfathomable grief. Thank you, Jesus.

# 12
# No Help

As the parents and siblings of a severe anorexic, we had no offers of help from any of the so-called authorities (as has been outlined) and perhaps the most disappointing and profoundly concerning of all was that we had no support from CAMHS themselves, who seemed to operate somewhat standoffishly and agencies that exists whatsoever throughout. Our GP did not offer us any kind of help in the form of counselling, support groups or anything. There was equally no support offered via Dr Crook and the hospital (in fact the opposite was the case as they seemed not really interested in us as the family at all).

This to my mind confirms more of what I was saying previously as regards the official system of dealing with mental health as being somewhat antiquated and not really operating in the twenty-first century. We were going through a lengthy trauma ourselves but with no support from any agencies whatsoever. It is very much wake-up time in this regard to my mind.

Yet there are agencies offering help: Why weren't we told about them? The agency 'Beat' offers a great deal of help. It has active helplines 24/7, student-lines and youth-lines. Their service is all confidential and contact can even be done via email.

There is also the organisation 'ABC' – Anorexia, Bulimia Care and another organisation somewhat ironically called 'F.E.A.S.T.' all offering support and help. But why were we never informed about these by our GP or the hospital or CAMHS, but instead made to feel so isolated and alone in dealing with this excruciating ordeal?

We struggled on ourselves and were truly blessed to have each other for comforting purposes and prayer.

# 13

# "Why...Sarah?"

The question was on everyone's lips.

I asked her what had made her do what she had done and she told me that the trigger had been a boy at school who had commented to her that she looked a 'bit chubby' one day. It was true that Sarah had just a little bit of pre-adolescent puppy fat on her at that time but nothing to speak of and was always a fit and active school and outside school sports team player.

Ironically, that same boy had apparently told her at school when seeing her in her anorexic state, "I really hope I didn't have anything to do with this, I'm so very sorry if I did!" (Yes, you did lad...so watch your words next time.)

I also asked her at another point what had made her do what she did (?) She told me that by eating virtually nothing like that, it made her feel that she had gotten full control over her food and that she was in control, as opposed to the food being in control over her.

The irony of course was that she had been totally out of control and had nearly killed herself in the process! I could see where she was coming from however.

Sarah began her slow process of physical, mental and emotional recovery and so did the rest of us. Praise God, we still had her with us. But by the complete Grace of God. Thank you, Jesus. Thank you. Hallelujah!

# 14

# Return from Death's Door

The next six months saw a fairly rapid turnaround for Sarah. She was now embarking full-on on a mission to prove to everyone that there hadn't been much wrong with her, to save face and to come back with a vengeance. She had gained adequate weight now, her hair was growing back slowly and properly and she had now even begun to jog again. That grit and determination which was central to her core was going to turn the balance around come what may.

Back at school, she took it by storm and achieved a completely astonishing year academically, in sport and in drama and theatre, as was her mission.

The West Buckland School Presentation of Prizes for the year to Sept 2015 shows her name dotted everywhere for awards and prizes:

1. Not only did she come back and win the Senior girls end of year Cross Country race (*'The Exmoor Run'*) in a record time.
2. She was one of only four to gain scholarship for her high GCSE grades; gaining all grade A's and A Stars, the *Shepherd Law for Prize for Scholarship.*

3. *The Gold Award for Maths Challenge.*
4. *Grade eight Gold Award for Acting.*
5. *The Headmaster's Award for Most Promising Senior Performer in Year 10–13.*
6. *The Festival Shield for Best Shakespeare Solo Performance for under 18 years.*
7. *The Cup for Best Dramatic Solo Performance for under 18 years.*
8. Awards for her Netball Team.
9. Out of school Netball team awards for Best Player etc.

These were just her main achievements for that year.

The biggest and best achievement was of course carried out by God, by the true grace and compassion of God, the sparing of her life.

We as her family, still continue to heal from this ordeal bit by bit. To reflect back and even to talk about this experience still hurts.

As I write this, Sarah is of a perfectly normal weight. She has a good job and is studying for a degree in psychology. She declined to write her part for this book. We love her and thank God that she is still with us today. All praise and glory be to God through whom all things are possible.

Michael Prentice

# Anorexia
## Additional account by Olivia Prentice, elder sister of Sarah

Olivia Prentice lives and works in Southampton, having obtained a B.A. Hons degree in Psychology some years ago. Since that time, she has worked on several projects for the Christian organisation 'Latin Link' whose mission it is to go to the poorer and developing countries to help them build schools, plant crops, and build good relations with the countries etc. Latin Link has taken her to South Africa, Kenya, Peru and soon to Brazil. She also carried out the role as Church pastoral liaison between a Southampton Church and the university and is currently helping others who are suffering from addictions in a full time role. In her spare time Olivia is a sporty young woman who enjoys going to the gym and marathon running.

Firstly, I want to begin by saying that Sarah is the best sister to me in the world, she always has and always will be the best sister anyone could ask for and her experience with anorexia does not and will not ever change that. I love her more than she will ever know and always will.

I was completing my A levels when Sarah got very ill. I remember sensing for a few months that she didn't seem herself and knew that she was losing weight quite dramatically. I remember a boy in her year group calling her 'fat' and it really affected her, she then began dieting which then spiralled out of control. A lot of girls at my school at the time also went on these strange diets and to me some of them would almost compete to eat the healthiest, even in my year group which was a couple of years above my sister's. This was concerning to me and combined with media pressures to look good from a young age I now know this is a recipe for disaster. What seemed like just a diet to me at first quickly spiralled out of control and I believe that the devil entered her mind and things quickly spiralled out of control. Next thing I knew, she was then in hospital as her weight had dropped a lot and both doctors and my parents were very concerned about her.

I think her hospital admission was what made me realise something serious was happening. I don't think I knew the extent of what was going on mentally or physically really though with Sarah at this time. I remember her looking quite pale, looking very thin and also her seeming quite distant, lacking many emotions and her hair getting very thin. I know my parents had taken her to the doctor's and very quickly it had been escalated to a hospital admission as there was a serious concern for her and that if there wasn't intervention, things could have ended very badly. I remember finding out that she was going to the hospital but not really registering it, if that makes sense. Next thing I knew, she was in the hospital with bare essentials. I remember thinking that they would just check her over, monitor her for a day or so and then tell her what she needed to do in order to get better. This definitely wasn't what happened. I remember being told that it was going to be more than just a day in the hospital and that's when I think I properly realised something was quite wrong. I then thought that surely it wasn't that bad, maybe she'll be in for a week or so and then be fine, it wasn't that serious was it she'd just lost a bit of weight. Again, I was wrong it was going to be way longer than a week that she would be there for. As her stay in the hospital got longer and longer and there wasn't a date that she would come out given, I grew more and more concerned – How could they not know how long she would be in for I thought, and surely all she had to do was eat properly for a few weeks, put on weight and then leave again? I now know how anorexia is way more complex than just gaining weight and being fine again.

As time progressed, she was still in hospital and was being constantly monitored by doctors, I would go to visit her in the evenings after my lessons and then return to school the next day as if nothing had happened. When I saw her in hospital, it scared me, I don't like that kind of environment anyway but seeing her there worried me a lot, I wondered what had happened, what had caused her to diet to such extremes, would she get better, when would she get better, would it take years? She was formally diagnosed with anorexia nervosa and her treatment began, however, all I really knew about anorexia nervosa was that it was about losing a lot of weight. However, not many people know the other severe physical and mental components of this illness. As I knew very little about the illness, I definitely knew very little about the treatment and recovery. I did, however, know that it could be life-threatening and was therefore very worried. I hoped that my sister just had it mildly and not severely but in the early stages, I definitely didn't realise how severely she had it.

At school people began to ask questions, I didn't know what to say. The first few weeks I remember just saying, "Oh, she's just ill, or not very well" but I knew soon I would have to say something else the longer it continued. I wanted to protect my little sister and her image which at the school was so so good. She was a high achiever, known for her strong desire and motivation to succeed. She was known as frequently top of her class and a strong member of many sports teams etc. She was known for constantly being top and I know that she put a lot of pressure on herself in order to achieve so highly. She was also a very popular girl, with lots of friends and a very sociable character. I wanted to respect her by not letting the whole world know what was going on. I also didn't like lying to people and found that hard. I told people she had an illness that was making her lose lots of weight but the doctors didn't know what it was and that they were doing tests to find out, they thought it was something to do with her small intestine. I knew the truth but didn't or couldn't say it. Some people asked how she was, they told me they hoped she would get better soon, so did I. Some people didn't know what to say to me, they knew I wasn't myself and was finding it hard to concentrate but I don't think they had the words or thought it was better to just leave me. I knew I looked very numb, often distant and much stressed. This continued throughout her time in the hospital. I was genuinely concerned and felt like I had to just be okay and try to continue like normal as best as I could.

One of my A level subjects ironically was psychology, I went into one lesson and the teacher explained that we would be talking about anorexia nervosa, I wanted to leave the room instantly but I knew I couldn't. If I did would people realise what was going on, would they think it was something I struggled with in the past, who knows. What I did know is that I needed to be in that lesson; I couldn't shy away from it. I needed to try and understand more about what was going on but it was tough. I wondered whether people would be able to tell something was going on even by the looks on my face but I did it and was so glad I did afterwards. What a lot of people don't know is about the theories behind anorexia nervosa and what causes it. There are many theories, some linking to childhood, others looking at biological dispositions and some focusing on social influences. What is also clear as that a lot of theories talk about personality types that may make you more susceptible to other influences. For example, personalities that care about others opinions more are more likely to be influenced by comments on their weight, or those with a lower self-esteem are more likely to be influenced by the images in the media etc. I encourage anyone reading this to find out more about anorexia, you never know who God may place in your path and it is important to equip yourself at least with basic knowledge about lots of different mental health disorders, especially as they are on the rise.

For many people, anorexia nervosa just appears as someone wanting control over their weight and taking control of their eating habits to the extreme, however, if you are reading this, I challenge you to understand that it is an extremely complex disorder. I ask that you to learn about it and to speak to people who have or are still experiencing it. No experience will be the same and I believe that the stigma surrounding eating disorders is huge and often people base their beliefs of anorexia not on fact but on what they have perhaps heard in the media only. Anorexia is also on the rise and I believe we all have a responsibility to educate ourselves and to learn how to support those who may be suffering from it. It is so much more than someone losing a bit too much weight.

So to return to the story as it were – I remember the numerous discussions my parents had with doctors about Sarah. I know that it was a very challenging time for them, one where they had to be extremely strong for us all as a family. I know there were difficult conversations for them and I know that they always had my sister's best interest at heart. They fought to ensure that she got the help she needed but they also were in some very difficult situations where what they believed was best for her was not always what the doctors were saying; a position that I will never know how difficult it was. In all honesty, I believe that the doctors were doing what they believed to be right, however, I question their ability to see Sarah for the beautiful, amazing girl she is at points. She was not just a number on the scales but a human with emotions who was hurting. I know Sarah's experience in the hospital was very mixed for her too, there were some nurses who were incredible in the way they treated her and some who failed to respect her as a person in terms of her privacy etc. My prayer is that every nurse and medical professional would respect each patient for the person they are and see through the condition or illness they may be experiencing. In the same token, I thank the medical professionals for the role they played in my sister's recovery and for acting swiftly in helping her to get back on her feet.

I want to return to my parents briefly: I know this experience affected them greatly as it would any parent. I believe the strength they both showed was immense and I thank God that Sam, Sarah and I have them as parents because they are both amazing. I know this experience was draining emotionally for both of them, and very challenging at points with trying to look after my brother and me, ensure Sarah was okay, and communicate with medical professionals, whilst also trying to stay sane themselves individually and as a couple. I know the doctors were very matter of fact with them and I pray that any other family who goes through something like this remains united despite the challenges, as we did. I also know my parents did extremely well, no parent is trained as it were for something like this and they took each challenge as it came and kept pushing through. I also admire and love my brother a lot, he was at quite a young age when this happened but that doesn't make him immune to emotions and the challenges that he had to face too and I am in awe of him and the man he has become. I am also extremely proud of my sister, no one will ever know or completely understand the inner demons she had to face during this experience and I am proud of her immensely for facing them head-on and not giving up when things were tough.

I also want to speak about my faith in relation to my experiences. I have been a Christian since about a year before this experience. My faith was definitely tested at points during this experience and has been in many ways since but I thank God for being my rock in this experience and many experiences since. There were times when I doubted God and wondered where he was, in particular, there was a specific moment when I remember looking at my sister when she was in her onesie at the hospital and I felt an immense wave of sadness, I wondered if she was going to get better at all and I really just wanted her to be okay within an instant but knew deep down it was going to be a process. I believe that God healed my sister, yes doctors etc were used as a part of that process but I believe that only God can completely heal both physically and mentally. I thank God too for being by my side through this experience and know that being able to pray and speak to him was a life changer for me. He knows your heart and the situations you may be facing, I feel like he wants me to remind someone of that today.

I want to focus a bit on the mental side rather than the physical side of anorexia nervosa. Many people have described that it is to do with control, often when other things in a person's life feel a bit out of control they seek to control their food and eating habits. I believe the devil is a part of this and negative voices that people may hear. I believe that he seeks to destroy and that the mind can be a huge way he tries to access people. I believe the devil can try to influence people's thought about themselves, in terms of how they view themselves and their overall thought patterns. In the case of anorexia nervosa, I believe that the devil may enter by telling people they are not good enough, perhaps that their life is not worth living, telling them they don't need to eat or that they should feel guilty if they eat. I believe that negative thoughts or voices are extremely dangerous and whether you believe that it is the devil or not, I know that negative thoughts or voices can spiral very quickly and can lead to self-destruction through disorders such as anorexia nervosa but also through suicide etc. I believe that it is important to try and recognise negative thoughts or voices and to confront them. For me personally, I believe the biggest weapon against the devil and his destruction is prayer and always will be prayer. In my sister's case, there were a lot of people both praying directly with her and for her but even from a distance and I believe prayer is powerful and did make all the difference.

I also believe that treatment for mental health illnesses needs to be more focused on the mind and therapy too and how to fight the devil as well as the physical recovery that needs to happen too in order to see progress and complete recovery. Mental health issues are mental and physical problems and need to be addressed in this way.

I also want to talk about support, and the importance of the people you surround yourself with. For me, there were definitely times where I felt like I couldn't talk to anyone about what was going on. I was at a private school where I didn't have a lot of friends already and the few friends I had were very focused on their work, which is not surprising as we were completing our A levels! I struggled with what was going on and to be honest, didn't really talk to anyone about it properly. I didn't know how to speak to my close friends about it and didn't tell them the extent of what was really happening, I didn't want people at school knowing exactly what was going on, so that rules out going to any teachers or my personal tutor, and I didn't want to burden my parents too much as I knew they were dealing with the situation head-on and my brother was still quite young at this time and I knew my parents were looking after him a lot too, especially as he couldn't be left in the house on his own etc. I very much had to keep my emotions under control at school and continue as normal and then tried to keep them together when I went to visit my sister in the hospital; I knew I had to be strong for her, for my brother and for my parents. I remember a couple of times distinctly where I took myself into the toilets at school on my break just so I could cry, without being seen by anyone whilst knowing I really needed to just let it out.

I encourage anyone who may have an experience like mine to find friends they can be very honest with, I'm not blaming mine as I feel like A levels are an extremely stressful time as it is and I also think some of them just didn't know what to say to me, partly because I wasn't telling them everything but partly because they didn't know how to be there for me, however, I think this experience taught me the importance of friends and finding a way to be completely honest with your close friends.

I know that one key person in my sister's recovery story was a girl named Roz. Roz was in the hospital bed alongside my sister throughout her time in the hospital. Like Sarah, Roz was in the hospital for mental health reasons and I know she had made attempts to kill herself in the past. Roz and Sarah formed one of the most beautiful bonds I have ever seen in my life and it was one slight beautiful thing in a very dark situation. They were of a similar age and you could see how well they got on. They would spend time watching movies together and just chatting and I know that God placed Roz there in the hospital with my sister as they supported each other through their tough times.

For me, this experience also showed me a lot about loving others, sometimes we want to be the ones who can control and change things but ultimately, that is not always what we can be. For me, I couldn't change the fact that my sister was in hospital unwell by my own strength. I had to just keep loving her, keep showing up for her and keep supporting her as best as I could. Love is a very powerful thing that we often underestimate. She needed to know that she was loved regardless of what was going on. Don't get me wrong as frustration, sadness, fear and tiredness were all a part of this process and they are normal emotions that I believe are important and important not to block too. I had to pretend to be immune to them at points but I can tell you the times when I could be still and be honest with God were the ones that were most valuable. You can only block emotions to a certain point ultimately they need to be processed and dealt with.

I also want to talk about patience. Patience was needed during this process. There were so many times I wanted my sister to be okay the next day but realistically that was never going to happen. Recovery from mental health illnesses just like sports injuries takes time. I believe God taught me a lot about patience during this time as I think I had very much got used to rushing around and just living my life, complaining about waiting ten minutes for buses when really waiting isn't always a bad thing and there is a lot of time for reflection, helping others etc. during the waiting.

I feel like my concept of time during this period of my life was very strange, to be honest, it seemed like the days went quickly in some ways as I was still busy with normal life but also dragged immensely at times as days turned into weeks and weeks to months as I wondered when she would be okay. It also feels strange looking back now in the sense of it was a chunk of my teenage years but also such a small fragment of my overall life and a lot has happened and changed since. I've been to university, travelled a lot and no longer even live in Devon etc. Looking back I know that God has used this experience to equip me for a lot of things since and to help ignite a huge passion in me for mental health and helping others. It is really cool to see how he pieces the puzzle together of our lives and how he uses our experiences for good. Whilst Sarah was in the hospital, I learnt a lot about myself, my emotions, my strengths and weaknesses and my ability to endure which had helped me massively.

I remember my parents wanting Sarah to leave the hospital as she really wasn't happy there and wanted to be at home and the doctors had kept making false promises about when she would be able to leave near the end of her hospital stay. They kept saying oh if she puts on X amount of kg by the end of the week we'll let her leave, then she would and they would then say oh another X amount of kg and then we will and this process kept repeating which was frustrating for everyone. I remember finding out she had eventually come home and was so glad. I knew she wasn't completely out of the woods but I knew it was a huge leap in the right direction. She still had to see the doctors for a few months in order to have her weight monitored and ensure she didn't start dropping it again because she had gone home and thought she could get away with it again.

The next thing I remember is her being back at school. I know she was very keen to get her reputation back as it were. I know she also struggled to settle back in as she was worried about other people's perceptions of what had happened and although most were fairly oblivious some still had their questions or doubted the stories I had come up with and she was worried they would find out the truth. I think she spoke to a couple of her very close friends (of whom some are still her friends today) about what had happened. I don't know what she has or hasn't told them but that isn't something I need to know. The next year at school she worked extremely hard to get good grades and to prove herself to people, for example, in the annual cross country run she did extremely well and placed very highly. Over time, things returned to normal and no one asked anything anymore. I know she wanted to turn things around quickly which is not surprising and I think she did so in a very quick time. I am also glad that she had a few very close friends who were really there for her and still are now.

I then finished my A levels and took a gap year. I knew I needed a break before university for a number of reasons and so spent the year volunteering overseas and working. To me, that year often feels like a blur because I was just living in the moment and was the first time I had been away from home by myself. I continued to strengthen my relationship with God and learn about myself whilst having a great time being abroad. I then returned the following year and started my studies at Southampton University where I studied psychology. Anorexia nervosa did come up in my course and it still reminded me of what had happened, however, this time I was able to look back on it as something in the past. I also was reminded of how important it is to educate yourself on mental health illnesses and my passion for helping others was fuelled even more. My course overall was amazing and I learnt so much as well as made a few close friends at this time and have stayed in Southampton since. I still don't know exactly where I'm heading but I know that God places me exactly where he wants me and I feel he wants me to come alongside others in all sorts of situations whatever they may be, to shine a light and to be a support for those around me.

After leaving university, I secured a job working as a student ministry assistant at Highfield Church in Southampton for a year part-time and I combined this with waitressing at Pizza Hut which I had been doing alongside my degree. I have been surrounded by incredible people here in Southampton which I am so grateful for. My year, as a student ministry assistant, involved lots of amazing things. I was responsible for organising a number of student events, such as bonfire nights, student meals and weekends away etc. but also for the pastoral side of students. I was involved in mentoring students on a one-to-one level, often catching up for coffee in cafes and getting to know a lot of students on a very deep personal level. I was able to be the one they could talk to about anything and everything which was very rewarding. The role was also challenging as a number of issues arose for the students I worked with which were quite tough but I was blessed to have an amazing team around me who could help me to help them. A variety of mental health issues were also prevalent and it was both a challenge and joy to be able to support students in getting and receiving help. Student mental health issues are vast and it is an important group of people that need to be supported.

As part of my role as a student ministry assistant, I was also able to lead a seminar on mental health and about looking after yourself and others with lots of group discussion which was a huge privilege and help to organise a talk on eating disorders led by https://familymentalwealth.com/who are a family who shares their experience of their daughter's anorexia with people across the country. To me, this talk was incredible as it was amazing to see a family so willing to share their experience and I know it had a huge impact on the students that heard it at Highfield Church as many spoke to me about it. Elizabeth (The daughter) has also written a book called *Life Hurts: A doctor's personal journey through anorexia* which to me was incredibly inspiring. I know that conversations about mental health are so important no matter what age you are, where you live, where you work etc. And I think it's important not to underestimate the impact sharing your experience can have on others.

In terms of my future, I'm currently working and about to become a mental health first aider before going to Brazil for a year (hopefully) and then I am looking to return to do some further training with the view to working in the charity sector or pastoral role in the future. I believe all of my experiences have shaped me into who I am today and I pray that I would continue to have open eyes to those around me and can continue to be there for others. I think there is a real danger of us being glued to our phones and not having deep meaningful conversations and really checking how people are and once the pandemic subsides again, I hope that we can all look to physically being there for others whilst in the meantime continue to support others from a distance. I also hope and continue to work on my own balance of looking after myself and others as both are important and pray that God continues to teach me how to do that well.

Olivia Prentice

This is Sarah today